The Art of Getting Through

Meaghan Tully

BookLeaf Publishing

India | USA | UK

Presentation by *BookLeaf Publishing*

Web: www.bookleafpub.com

E-mail: info@bookleafpub.com

ISBN: 9789363310988

First edition 2024

*For all of the incredible people who have been
a part of my recovery.*

*To my sweet daughter, Charlotte, may you only
inherit my sparkle and joy.*

PREFACE

Life as I knew it was coming to an end when I was finally admitted into residential treatment for my eating disorder. But the wars I fought with myself did finally end. For years I couldn't stand myself, until one day, I could.

Selfish.

And here we are we look up tips
It's fine it's fine it's just a slip
It's just a slip it's just a sip
you only brought it to your lips
Once or twice or three times max
Or fuck it have another glass
It doesn't matter it won't take long
Selfish stupid and fucking wrong.

Selfish.
Selfish.

Revolve my world around coming for you but
all it was
was selfish.

Self
time money needy
insecure unsure
never enough too much
ish

Watch the life refill your eyes
 but suddenly they drain.
You
Deserve

The
Fucking
Pain.

Falling backwards paint your arms
Feel attention ignore the harm
Selfish.

Not a single thought of your own
Selfish.

Secret life and twisted lies
With razors to your arms and thighs
Attention please attention here
The desperate one the one in tears
Selfish.

You know it's wrong
You know it's cruel
My God are you a fucking fool
Selfish.

And here we are all said and done
Well isn't this just so much fun
Selfish.

You lose yourself, let yourself go
Pathetic pain yet still you know
He loves every version and he'll never leave

Despite the fucked up paths you weave
Selfish.

I can't do it anymore I'll go insane
The casualties of war inside my brain
I deserve the hurt and weight I've gained
I deserve it
All the pain
And I can't even speak its name
Just rip it out leave no remains
You're not a victim you're to blame

Everything you do and say
God just make it go away
The world gets worse each moment you stay
Don't burden them another day

You being here is so
Fucking
Selfish.

Selfish.
Selfish.

But still you sit upon your throne
When you just deserve to be alone
Just imagine if they would've known.

You are so fucking selfish.

Hopeless Cause.

I'm a fuck up
and it shows.
Can't do anything right
and everyone knows.

Broken rules
and stupid behavior
"Get your shit together"
I will, I will later.

Disappointment, sneaking, lies
I couldn't be more wrong.
And when nobody believes in me
it's pretty hard to stay strong.

I'm a terrible patient
a terrible friend
a burden to everyone
and it never ends.

Go ahead, rally up
tell me all my flaws
gang up on me, tear me down,
don't even take a pause.

Hey, why not call my parents?
Let them join the fun
Tell them I'm a hopeless cause.
Pass around the gun.

Everyone I love so much
I thought they felt the same
But all I've done is fuck it up
and they think that I'm insane.

I get it, I'm wrong
Tell me a million more times.
I'm fully aware that I'm no good.
At this point call it crime.

I say I'll change,
but you just laugh
I say it's just a slip
You say it's my path.

I'll just sit there
shaking while I cry
I'll just sit and take the blows
and really want to die.

If humiliation's what you want,
Congrats, you won the prize.
I'll dwell on all the harm I've done
I'm a fuck up, no surprise.

I really thought I was trying
but I guess that's not the case.
Only focus on the bad I guess
and you control the pace.

Maybe I should stay away
I'll never rise above.
You think I want to make things hard,
but all I want is love.

Trapped.

Trapped.
There is
no
way
out.

Trapped.
in a torture chamber hell.
Escaping isn't possible.
She's fallen down the well.

Every feature, every inch
She can't stand another day.
Disgraceful, shame-ridden, way too much
God, please take her away.

She takes a razor, takes a pin,
she takes her jagged nails
she wants to take the pain away
but all she does is fail.

She shoves her fingers down her throat
she rids herself of fear.
It's killing her. She's dying.
But she'd rather disappear.

Binge and purge and starve yourself
slice your pathetic arms
you'll never be enough for me;
for that you must be harmed.

Trapped.
You stupid girl.
You're nothing but a size.
Ugly, vile, fat fat fat
It's no wonder that you cry.

What's next?
You wretched girl
those pounds don't suit you well.
Just purge and starve and cut yourself.
You're trapped.
You're trapped
in
hell.

Falling.

Falling again back into he hell that once
consumed me
Faster by the second
eating me alive
breath by breath
moment by moment
Every step I take, it takes a bigger one
Every word I say, it says a meaner one
It, not he
Focus. Remember.
It.
It is not a human. It cant have the control
But it won't stop trying
I'm running low on power
I don't think I have it in me to keep fighting
It might just be so much better
If there's less of me, more of it
I try or I die trying
Or maybe
I just
Die.

Hurt.

She smiles at the people
She loves to make them laugh.
They think that she's so happy
They smile on her behalf.

But late at night when she's alone,
The smile's done her harm.
It hides the things she really feels,
but then you see her arm.
And her ankles.
And her legs.
And her hips.

The scars consume her everywhere
you'd think she'd feel the pain.
Her mind is telling her it's good;
it's driving her insane.

She takes her razors, takes her tools
she rips herself apart.
Finally, it makes her feel,
but not what's in her heart.

There's something that it does for her
it makes her feel alive.

Emotions numbed, cravings met,
and off of that she thrives.

When will it end?
The pain just feels so good.
Others say it's got to stop
she doesn't think it should.

Maybe if someone loved her,
maybe if she tried,
maybe if she gave herself a chance,
there'd be nothing left to hide.

It's Back

When did breathing
Become
So
Fucking
Hard?
It's back
It's back.
It has its arms around me
wrapped so tightly
so securely
a feeling of acceptance I've never felt before
with anyone
or anything
It likes me
even when I'm not sure if anyone else does
It always wants to be with me
around me
a part of me
all of me
And now
I am
Willing.

Fine.

It's fine.
It's fine that you don't love me.
It's fine.
Neither do I.

I'm worthless anyway
I'm pushy and annoying
I try too hard to get your love
When it's love that I'm destroying.

It's fine that you don't love me
Everything is fine.
I'll sleep it off, fake a grin
Everything is fine.

How could someone love me anyway?
I sure as hell don't.
You've made it clear that I'm too much
so now I just won't.

I won't give myself to you
I'll bottle up my love.
I guess some people care too much
and I am number one.

It's just not worth the hurt I feel
to be so full of love
No one loves ME. No one does.
I guess there's just nothing to love.

Sometimes I wonder what it'd be like
to have a heart of hate instead.
Maybe I wouldn't feel so unlovable
If hatred filled my head.

It's fine.
I'll just pretend I feel no pain.
It's fine. Really.
I'll just sit down in the rain.

Motivation? Ha, it never lasts
What an optimistic lie.
So blindly looking at your life
as if you want to try.

It's fine.
Don't love me.
I'm used to it by now.
You can stop pretending
Show's over, take a bow.

It's fine.

Tough Love.

Crawl into bed with all the things
you've been bottling up
and
suffer.

Turn off the light
lie down
and
just
fucking
cry.
Cry so hard.

Feel your body.
Cry harder.
Remember that there's tomorrow.
Cry so hard your body starts to ache.
Your chest tightens.
You're losing air
Your head throbs
Your heart barely gets enough oxygen.
Cry so fucking hard.

You are
so
fucking

fat.

You're disgusting.
Squeeze your stomach.
Feel your huge thighs.
Jiggle your flabby arms.
Foul, wretched little girl.
You die inside,
knowing that you can't
just
die.

You'll wake up and the torture of life
will beat you down
and make it hurt
for another day.

Wait for the elevator in the morning,
but stand by the rail.
Stare down over it.
Imagine diving head first
to your escape.
It's all right there.
Your one way ticket out of the hell you're living.
Jumping.

Elevator opens, go inside.
Time for another fucking day.
Get to the treatment center,

sleep, wake up, eat, sleep, repeat.
Feels like that's all it's good for.

Go back to the apartments,
look over the ledge,
and then go inside.
Look out your window.
What a fall.
If only the door could open.

It's almost time to cry again,
but a recovery coach comes to hug you.
Your roommate wants to play a game,
and the fish need to be cleaned.

You take pride in your ability to keep the fish
fed, clean, and happy.
You're the best fish mom here.
You've loved all your fish-
You didn't even know it was possible to love a
fish.
You still get sad when you think of ones who
died.

You still get sad when you think of your cat that
died
and your grandparents and family and friends
who have passed.

You claim that if you take that jump, no one
would feel that way.
They'll just get over it.
But you're not over the deaths of your loved
ones
even though they passed as early as fourth grade.
And you miss every little pet you've ever had.
Every fish, hamster, bunny, bird
You'll love them forever.

If you weren't here
would anyone experience that?
You feel like they wouldn't.
But I think you know better.
Can you imagine what you'd be doing to your
little sister?
That's fucked up.
Just because you despise yourself
to the point of physical pain,
would you really do that to your little sister?
Fuck no.
You wouldn't.
Man up.
You can't just cop out like that.
Even if you hate yourself,
at least
do it
alive.

You walk back into your bedroom,
but this time, you don't turn off the lights yet.
You look around for a moment.
There isn't an inch of your wall
that isn't covered in pictures,
drawings, letters, mail,
and all the little things people have given you.
You have two huge lists of why other patients
love you.
Who would take THAT much time out of their
day
if they didn't absolutely love you?
No one would.

Why can't you just fucking accept
that you are loved.
You are loved.
You are loved for your humor,
your support, your laugh, your ability to
connect,
and your huge heart that has room for the world.

No one fucking cares if your stomach rolls over
your pants when you sit.
No one fucking cares that your thighs touch
or that your arms jiggle
or that you have cellulite.
No one fucking cares.
So why do you?

What are you doing?
Look over that ledge
and be grateful there's a dumpster to collect
trash,
a sidewalk to walk on,
and birds to fill the trees.
Be thankful you even have a body.
A body that works, heals,
and puts up with your shit.

The point of existing,
no matter how much it hurts,
isn't to figure out a way to end it.

You're in so much pain.
You ache with hatred for yourself,
but you're still here.
Don't jump.
Find a way to stop the pain.
You have all the tools you need
right in front of your face.

You can't stand the way you look,
your arms are scarred,
you fucked up your bones,
and you're missing out on months of your life to
be here.
But that's the way it is.

There's nothing you can do
to change what's happened.
But the present
is your best friend.

Right now,
don't jump.
DO recognize the beauty of the world around
you,
DO change the subject when you're picking
yourself apart,
It's never going to change.
Let it go.

Don't jump.
Jump into life.
Jump with joy.
Jump over every hurdle.
Jump in place just because you can.

Don't jump because you think you should end it
all.

It's an option,
but in this moment,
don't do it.
Just
don't
do it.

Tomorrow.

Today was not the day
crying in a ball
wanting to escape from life
truly done with it all.

Today I was miserable.
Today I got bad news.
Today I couldn't smile.
Today I was confused.

But today is not the only day
As terrible as it seems
Today can come to an end
And you can have sweet dreams.

Tomorrow today is over
Tomorrow is round two
Tomorrow is its own day
Tomorrow depends on you.

The past is all that's happened,
It's what we cannot change.
But tomorrow is a brand new slate,
a chance to turn the page.

Tomorrow is a brand new start
to the book you call your life.
Tomorrow can be anything
anything you'd like.

Your past does not define you,
don't worry about your arms.
They're just as good for hugging
as you thought they were for harm.

How can this be different?
How can I be free?
Just rid myself of all the hate
the horrid hate of me.

Why do you despise yourself?
You hug and laugh and care
you have so much love to give the world
and your strife just isn't fair.

Tomorrow can be a brand new piece
some art you can create
but you won't paint with a razor
and you won't draw your self-hate.

Your arms are not for hurting
nor your ankles or your hips
they help you live your crazy life
don't let yourself be gipped.

Put down the razor.
Lay it down to rest.
Tell it that you're done for good
and that all it caused was stress.

You don't need to hurt yourself
or punish all your flaws
you deserve to show your beautiful arms
not limbs wrapped up in gauze.

Tomorrow can be the day
the wounds can start to heal
the day you can forgive yourself
the day you start to feel.

Tomorrow really isn't far
tomorrow's now today
Wipe your tears, crack a smile,
today will be your day.

haiku1.

25

If you aren't here
tomorrow, the world will ache.
You are meant to stay.

If you aren't here
tomorrow, the world will ache.
You are meant to stay.

haiku2.

Your skin is fragile
yet resilient and strong.
Treat it as your home.

haiku3.

Stopping in her tracks
she took a look around her.
What a joy to live.

haiku4.

Please do not get stuck
in the depths of the darkness.
You were born the light.

haiku5.

How beautiful that
the sun rises each morning
knowing what she's worth.

haiku6.

30

Don't ignore the way
starlight twinkles through your eyes
Your magic is real.

Wrapping Paper

Sometimes there was no time,
And that was OK.
The party theme was rainbows,
But she wrapped the gift in gray.

On Mother's Day she discovered
Only one choice in the house
The stunning necklace wrapped up tight
With baby Mickey Mouse.

On Father's Day the opposite-
She'd used up all the blue.
The first gift from their baby boy
Wrapped in ballerina shoes.

Her best friend threw a baby shower,
But Christmas time was near
"Can't wait to meet your little one!"
Wrapped in candy canes and deer.

She was a bridesmaid in a wedding
That snuck up way too soon
The only bag she had for them
Said "happy birthday" on balloons.

Then one day it was her turn,
But she was ashamed of what she saw.
The mirror seemed to pick out
Every single flaw.

Pick an outfit, do her hair,
Get ready for her friends
But somehow all the things she saw
Just never seemed to end.

This time the party was for her,
There was nothing to wrap.
She giggled as a tear rolled down,
Revisiting each wrapping mishap.

The paper, the bags, the mismatched bows
They all got the job done.
But the only part that mattered
Was watching them open every one.

Every gift was thoughtful,
A special thing from her.
All the silly wrapping jobs-
She could barely remember what they were.

If I get any gifts, she thought,
They could wrap them in saran.
She'd love them for the thought, the care,
And that they gave it 'cause they can.

So then she looked at all the clothes
She'd just thrown on the floor
And suddenly she realized
There just had to be more.

The wrapping never mattered
Nor your body, clothes, or shoes.
Maybe they'll all come today
Because the gift was always you.

Sparkle

To myself,

There are past versions of you that are carved into your memory like the Rosetta Stone of the intricacies of your being.

Versions that have been kicked to the ground, versions that just wanted to feel worthy, versions that bring you so much pain, and versions that made it through. But, maybe they belong there.

Maybe every up, down, and all-over-the-place has been carefully woven into the map that makes up you.

Sometimes you want to tear the map to shreds and run it over with a truck and throw it in a volcano and then run it over with a bigger truck just in case.
But what if you give it a chance to lead you where you want to go?

If you really, fully open up the map, you'll notice that little bit of glitter that won't come off the corner.

Ah, your sparkle.

Like glitter, no matter how hard you try or how
many ways you attempt to, you just cannot get
rid of it.
Your sparkle is like that, too.

You can fight it all you want, but even in the
worst versions of yourself, your sparkle was
there, too.
Even if it was just that one last speck of glitter.
That relentless one.
You have that effect on people.

No matter what the circumstance, you've
changed everyone who has come into your life
in some way that can never be erased.

Meanwhile, you've spent so much time looking
for the right things to do, the key to being
worthy and loved, the secret to saving everyone,
the magic parts of life.

What if the magic is you?

What if your sense of humor, your kindness, and
your creativity are the magic?
What if the way you love so fiercely, so deeply,
and so much is the magic?

Your sparkle- maybe that's been the magic all
along.

Maybe every moment and every part of you
doesn't feel sparkly and magical, and that's okay.
It doesn't take it away.

Magic is amazing in that way.
Most people don't believe in it,
but the ones who do get to experience life in a
beautiful way that can't be explained.

Maybe you're like that, too.
Maybe you only need the beauty of the ones
who believe in you.

Your baby wakes up every morning calling,
"Mama!" and jumping for joy when you open
her door.
Her face immediately lights up with that
unbelievable smile and crazy hair and button
nose just because she gets to see you.
Straight out of bed, 100% natural and unaltered
you.
This sweet, innocent, pure, untainted soul looks
at you like you are the greatest thing in the
world.
Because you are.

The glitter on the map isn't fake.
The map of you is exactly what it is supposed to be.
The routes it took created every chapter of you.
Even if this chapter isn't your favorite, it's still a part of a pretty magical book.
Just turn the page, and you'll see the glitter that never left the bottom corner.

Maybe it's okay to be where you are. Maybe this is your time to figure it all out. Maybe you needed this long for all of it to process.
Maybe it isn't just a chapter.
Maybe we're on to Book 2.

Go ahead.
Begin your next route.
Write your new Chapter 1,
and start Book 2 however you want.

And don't forget to add some sparkle.

Love,
Me

One Sentence Letters to Really Shitty People

To the boy who told me that no one would ever love me,
my wedding vows disagree.

To the ones who said my invitations got "lost in the mail,"
I'm so glad they never came.

To the girl who said no one liked me because I was fat,
I'd hate to be liked simply for being thin.

To the boy who laughed when he found out I liked him,
I hope you have a better sense of humor now.

To the girls who excluded me from every single group,
You melted together while I learned to shine on my own.

To the girl who said I was trying to steal her thunder,

I was always the thunder. You are merely the
rain.

To the girl who can't just get over it,
It must be getting really lonely under it.

To the ones who refuse to let it go,
It must be getting so heavy to hold.

To the one who said my love was selfish,
you missed out on everything I had to give.

To the ones who talked behind my back,
there were far better things waiting in front.

To the ones who hid behind a screen,
I pity your cowardly attempt to feel in control.

To the boy who used me and tore me apart,
I am so glad that my pieces are new.

To the one who said I'm "psychotically clingy,"
I'm so thankful I ripped myself away from you.

To the one who manipulated me because I was
fragile,
my foundation still remains strong.

To the boy who led me on because he could,
thank God I finally changed directions.

To the best friend who chose him over me,
I hope you've learned to make better decisions.

To the boy who let me go,
Thank you. I never would have walked away.

To the boy who loved me but then chose her,
I hope her looks were really so worth it.

To the woman who threw me to the wolves and
blamed me for getting bitten,
you still howl at the moon while I bask in the
sun.

To the ones who make me feel like I have to
prove my worth,
you will never decrease my value.

To the one who chose them until they stopped
choosing you,
the years you lost of ME can never be regained.

To the ones who only cared about my body,
you never deserved my beautiful mind.

To those who praised me as I withered away,
the only weight I needed to lose was you.

But,
To the little girl who didn't want to live,
I'm so glad that you did.